ESIDENTS
*and*
RST LADIES

# JAMES & DOLLEY
# MADISON

By

Ruth Ashby

WORLD ALMANAC® LIBRARY

Please visit our web site at: www.worldalmanaclibrary.com
For a free color catalog describing World Almanac® Library's list of high-quality books
and multimedia programs, call 1-800-848-2928 (USA) or 1-800-387-3178 (Canada).
World Almanac® Library's fax: (414) 332-3567.

Library of Congress Cataloging-in-Publication Data

Ashby, Ruth.
    James & Dolley Madison / by Ruth Ashby.
        p. cm — (Presidents and first ladies)
    Includes bibliographical references and index.
    ISBN 0-8368-5757-7 (lib. bdg.)
    ISBN 0-8368-5763-1 (softcover)
    1. Madison, James, 1751-1836—Juvenile literature.  2. Madison, Dolley, 1768-1849—Juvenile literature.
3. Presidents—United States—Biography—Juvenile literature.  4. Presidents' spouses—United States—
Biography—Juvenile literature.  5. Married people—United States—Biography—Juvenile literature.
I. Title: James and Dolley Madison.  II. Title.
E342.A84    2005
973.5'1'092—dc22
[B]                                                                                          2004057739

JB
MADISON, J.
C. 1

First published in 2005 by
World Almanac® Library
330 West Olive Street, Suite 100
Milwaukee, WI  53132  USA

Copyright © 2005 by Byron Preiss Visual Publications, Inc.

Produced by Byron Preiss Visual Publications, Inc.
Project Editor: Kelly Smith
Photo Researcher: Larry Schwartz
Designed by Four Lakes Colorgraphics Inc.
World Almanac® Library editorial direction: Mark J. Sachner
World Almanac® Library editor: Jenette Donovan Guntly
World Almanac® Library art direction: Tammy West
World Almanac® Library graphic designer: Melissa Valuch
World Almanac® Library production: Jessica Morris

Photo Credits:
Library of Congress: 4 (top and bottom), 6, 8 (top), 10, 11, 12, 14, 15, 18, 19, 25, 27, 28, 38, 39; North Wind
Picture Archives: 21; The Granger Collection, New York: 5, 7 (top and bottom), 8 (bottom), 9, 16, 17, 22, 23,
26, 29, 31, 34, 35 (top and bottom), 37, 40, 42
Cover art: The Granger Collection, New York

Printed in Canada

1 2 3 4 5 6 7 8 9 09 08 07 06 05

# CONTENTS

Words that appear in the glossary are printed in
**boldface** type the first time they occur in the text.

# 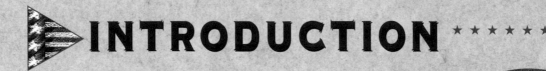INTRODUCTION

On Tuesday, August 23, 1814, the British army was advancing on Washington, D.C., and President James Madison was worried about leaving his wife, Dolley, by herself in the President's House. He had to depart for the battlefront to consult with his generals, as he told her. Did she have the "courage or firmness" to wait alone, with just a few servants, until his return? Staunchly, Dolley replied that she did.

Madison knew that he could depend on his wife without question, as she could depend on him. When they were first married in 1794, James and Dolley had seemed an unlikely couple. At nearly 5 feet 6 inches (168 centimeters), James was thin and frail-looking, forty-three years old and a longtime bachelor. The slightly taller Dolley, bursting with good health, was a twenty-six-year-old widow with a small child. He was brilliant, scholarly, and reserved in public; she was outgoing and generous, a real "people person." Yet they learned to love each other deeply, and Dolley's warmhearted personality and skills as a hostess proved indispensable as James made the climb from congressman to **secretary of state** and finally to president of the United States. For nearly forty-two years, James and Dolley Madison had a nearly perfect marriage of opposites.

James Madison, fourth president of the United States.

Dolley Payne Madison, first lady of the United States.

# CHAPTER ONE

# A GENTLEMAN AND A SCHOLAR

James Madison grew up on a tobacco plantation in Orange County in central Virginia, the first son of James Madison Sr. and Nelly Conway Madison. From the moment he was born on March 16, 1751, James Jr. was treated with the respect due the oldest son of one of the most influential and well-to-do families in the colony. His father managed an estate of about 5,000 acres (2,023 hectares) and owned approximately one hundred slaves. When James Jr. —known as Jemmy to distinguish him from his father—was nine, the family moved into a brand-new brick house on their plantation, which would later be known as Montpelier. Someday James would inherit it all.

Until he was eleven, James was educated at home with his nine brothers and sisters. Then, having read all the books in his father's study, he was sent about 70 miles (113 kilometers) away to study with a Scottish schoolteacher named Donald Robertson. "All that I have been in life I owe largely to that man," James said of Robertson later. Always a dedicated scholar, James learned French, Latin, Greek, geometry, algebra, history, and literature. Afterward, James went back to Montpelier for two years of private tutoring with his brothers and sisters and then on to college.

A wood engraving of Montpelier, the Madison's estate in Orange County, Virginia, completed in approximately 1760. James Madison Jr. was nine years old when his family moved into the new home, which began as a simple eight-room house.

When James set off for the College of New Jersey at Princeton, he was eighteen years old with a slender build that made him look even smaller than he was. All his life, James would suffer from delicate health—fever, stomach upsets, and falling spells that he later described as "sudden attacks, somewhat resembling epilepsy." Despite his fragile constitution, however, he studied so hard at Princeton that he finished both his junior and senior year course requirements in a single year.

Princeton awakened James's interest in the concept of religious freedom. Under the guidance of a Presbyterian minister named John Witherspoon, the college promised "free and equal liberty and advantage of education [to] any person of any religious denomination whatever." Such religious tolerance was unknown in pre-Revolutionary War Virginia, where the Anglican Church was the official government-supported church. All his life, Madison would be convinced that "Religious bondage shackles and debilitates the mind and unfits it for every noble enterprise, every expanded prospect." He would make the pursuit of religious freedom his life's work.

James arrived home in April 1772 and promptly collapsed from overwork. After he recovered, he didn't know what to do with the rest of his life. At first, he tried the study of law but soon gave it up as "coarse and dry." While he was casting about for a vocation, he became more and more involved in the rising conflict between Great Britain and its thirteen North American colonies.

James Madison in a miniature portrait painted by Charles Willson Peale, 1783. After graduating, Madison found his calling in Virginia politics. He soon gained national attention with his impressive record of service.

## A Rising Storm

The problem went back a decade. In 1763, Britain had won a nine-year war against France that was fought in North America for control of the Ohio River Valley. The French and Indian War was so expensive that the British Parliament decided to make the colonists pay part of its cost. It passed the Stamp Act of 1765, which required that all paper goods sold in the colonies—newspapers, legal documents, playing cards, and so on—had to bear a stamp proving that a tax had been paid on them. Because the colonies had no representatives in Parliament to approve the tax, colonists were furious. Declaring "no taxation without representation!" they refused to pay. Parliament was forced to repeal the Stamp Act, only to impose taxes on other goods such as glass, paper, and tea a few years later. With every new tax, organized resistance grew and **boycotts** of English goods increased.

Matters came to a head on December 16, 1773, when men and boys disguised as Mohawk Indians dumped chests of taxed tea into Boston Harbor. In retaliation, Britain dispatched additional troops to Boston and closed its port. Colonial leaders immediately organized a meeting of all the colonies, called the Continental Congress. When the congress met in September 1774, it urged the colonies to organize local military groups called **militias.**

As the oldest son of a prominent citizen, twenty-three-year-old Madison was commissioned as a colonel in the Orange County militia. He knew he was not strong enough to be a regular soldier—

The British government was surprised by the avalanche of colonial protest to the Stamp Act of 1765. Colonists not only refused to use the stamps, but also rioted and staged stamp burnings.

The Boston Tea Party was an act of colonial protest. Upset by the tax on tea, angry colonists threw 342 chests of tea belonging to the British East India Company into Boston Harbor.

Seven hundred British troops were met on Lexington Green by seventy-seven local minutemen. Someone, no one knows who, fired the first shot and a battle ensued. When the smoke cleared, eight Americans were dead. Only one British soldier was wounded.

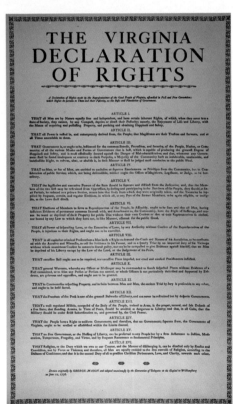

The Declaration of Rights to the Virginia Constitution, written by George Mason and adopted by the Virginia House of Delegates in Williamsburg on June 12, 1776.

and in fact he fainted during his first drill. However, he was eager to fight for his country. "We are very busy at present in raising men and procuring the necessities for defending ourselves and our friends in case of sudden invasion," he boasted to an old college friend.

Events moved fast. On April 19, 1775, colonial **minutemen** and British **redcoats** faced each other across the village green at Lexington, Massachusetts—and the American Revolution began. A month later, the second Continental Congress convened in Philadelphia and called upon Virginian George Washington to be commander in chief. He agreed and left for Boston to head the new Continental Army.

## A Stand for Independence

If Madison could not fight, he could still do what he did best—think. In May 1776, he was chosen to represent Orange County in the Virginia Convention, meeting in the state capital of Williamsburg. The convention was meeting to draw up a constitution and a declaration of rights for the new Virginia State

# The Thirteen Colonies

By 1732, thirteen English colonies stretched along the eastern coast of the North American continent. From north to south, they were Massachusetts (including present-day Maine), New Hampshire, Rhode Island, Connecticut, New York, Pennsylvania, New Jersey, Delaware, Maryland, Virginia, North Carolina, South Carolina, and Georgia. Although each colony had its own governor and legislative assembly, all the colonies were ruled from afar by Great Britain. When Britain went to war against France in North America in 1754–1763, colonial militia fought alongside the British Army. The French and Indian War forced the colonists to work together for their mutual protection and gave them a common identity as Americans. Within thirteen years after the war had ended, the thirteen colonies would assert their independence from Britain.

An eighteenth century map of the thirteen original American colonies.

government. Only twenty-five years old and inexperienced in legislative debate, Madison at first said little, deferring to George Mason, the primary author of the declaration. However, Madison had one very important contribution to make.

Mason's original draft said that the government would "tolerate" religious freedom. Madison, though, thought that personal religious beliefs were none of the government's business and that it had no right to "tolerate" anything. He proposed, and the convention accepted, the following change in wording: "All men are equally entitled to the free exercise of religion according to the dictates of conscience." In other words, people had a natural right to worship as they chose, a right that no government could take away from them.

Madison enjoyed his political experience so much that in April 1777 he decided to run for a seat in the new Virginia House of

Like Madison, Thomas Jefferson was an obsessive student, often spending fifteen hours of the day with his books, three hours practicing his violin, and the remaining six hours eating and sleeping.

Delegates. However, the young idealist violated established practice by not providing the traditional barrel of whiskey for voters at the polling place. They decided that young Madison was tightfisted and snobbish, and he lost the election.

Instead, Madison was appointed to serve on an executive board that advised the governor of Virginia. In June 1779, the new governor was Thomas Jefferson. From the beginning, the short, scholarly Madison and the tall, intellectually curious Jefferson were drawn to each other. They had much in common: a love of books, learning, the United States, religious freedom, natural history, and Virginia plantations. They shared a dislike of slavery, Great Britain, and **tyranny** of any kind. It was the start of a lifelong friendship.

In December 1779, James Madison was chosen as one of four Virginia delegates to the Continental Congress in Philadelphia. Although Madison was twenty-eight, he still looked exceptionally young. By then, he had adopted the uniform he would wear for the rest of his life: a black coat, breeches, and black silk stockings. When

## Madison and Slavery

James Madison grew up in a slave-holding family on a Virginia estate dependent on the labor of approximately one hundred slaves. While still a young man, he told his friend Edmund Randolph that he wanted to find a source of income that would "depend as little as possible on the labor of slaves." In his later years, he spoke to English writer Harriet Martineau about the issue. "In regard to slavery, [Madison] owned himself to be almost in despair," she wrote. He believed not only that slavery was inherently evil, but also that it threatened the very existence of the nation to which he had devoted his life. In the early 1800s, as Congress disputed the expansion of slavery into the western territories, the divide between the northern and southern states became deeper and more bitter. Yet after years of reflection, Madison never found a personal or national solution to the greatest problem the new nation faced.

Madison never freed his own slaves. In his will, he left them to his wife Dolley, with the caution, "None of them should be sold without his or her consent." In 1844, when Dolley's son Payne Todd threatened to sell the slaves to pay his debts, she sold Montpelier, the Madison plantation, rather than break up black families who had been living on the land for generations.

he rose to speak, his voice was barely audible. Madison was "no bigger than half a piece of soap," a fellow delegate declared. Over time, however, the delegates learned to rely on Madison's sharp mind and good judgment. In the eyes of many, his intellect made him a giant.

Madison was dismayed by the ineffectuality of the Congress. In Philadelphia, the delegates bickered and delayed, while on the battlefront, General Washington tried to organize a mob of underfed, badly clothed, homesick soldiers into an effective fighting force. Congress was wholly "dependent on the states," Madison wrote in disgust. "They can neither enlist, pay, nor feed a single soldier, nor execute any other purpose but as the means are first put into their hands." The Articles of Confederation, written by Congress in 1777 and ratified by the states in 1781, created a "firm league of friendship" among the states but gave the national government little real authority. It could not raise or collect taxes or regulate trade, and it had no chief executive to carry out laws. Madison spent a lot of time thinking about how to balance the power of a national government against the power of the individual states.

During his three years in Philadelphia, Madison lived in a boardinghouse with other congressional delegates. In 1783, he fell in love with the daughter of a fellow boarder, a vivacious sixteen year-old named Kitty Floyd. Despite the sixteen-year difference in their ages, she encouraged his courtship, and they became engaged. While away on summer vacation, however, she fell in love with a medical student closer to her own age. Kitty wrote James a farewell letter, admitting that she felt "indifferent" to him now, then sealed the letter with rye dough instead of sealing wax. James took the dough as a direct insult. Upset and humiliated, he would not court another woman for ten years.

A portrait of Catherine "Kitty" Floyd from 1783.

Meanwhile, with the help of French troops, Washington's decisive victory against the British at Yorktown, Virginia, in 1781 had won the war for the United States. Although a formal peace treaty was not signed until 1783, the Revolutionary War was over.

George Washington (front row, second from left) accepts the surrender of British general Charles Cornwallis (front row, second from right) at Yorktown, Virginia. Although both men appear in this image, in reality, Cornwallis claimed illness and sent his second-in-command. In return, Washington let his second-in-command accept the surrender.

Madison's term limit was also up in 1783, and he returned to the Virginia legislature. There, he kept a close eye on the national political scene. As the new United States stumbled through the first years of independence, the Articles of Confederation proved even weaker than he had feared. Among other problems, the nation had no way to repay its war debts and no way to settle disputes between states. In 1786, Madison, Alexander Hamilton of New York, and other national leaders decided that something had to be done. They called for a national convention to amend the Articles of Confederation.

Throughout the spring of 1787, Madison energetically prepared for the meeting, studying books on government, trade, and history. Madison realized that merely revising the articles would not be enough. The United States needed a whole new constitution.

## Father of the Constitution

When the Constitutional Convention opened in the Philadelphia State House on May 25, 1787, James Madison took a seat at the front of the hall. Though the meetings were held in secret, Madison made himself responsible for keeping a record of the proceedings. "I was not absent a single day no more than a fraction of an hour in any day so that I could not have lost a single speech, unless a very short one," he remembered later. At night, by candlelight, Madison transcribed and completed his notes. It was a monumental effort.

On May 29, Edmund Randolph of Virginia presented Madison's grand plan to the rest of the Convention. The "Virginia

Plan," as it is known, was a radical change from the Articles of Confederation. It called for a strong national government with three branches: the legislative, the executive, and the judicial. The legislative branch would make the laws; the executive branch, headed by a president, would carry out the laws; and the judicial branch would decide if the laws were being carried out fairly. Under the Virginia Plan, the legislature would be divided into two houses, and both would be chosen on the basis of state population.

Immediately, delegates from the small states objected. William Paterson of New Jersey proposed a single legislative house, in which each state would have just one vote. For weeks, the delegates argued. Finally, Roger Sherman of Connecticut came up with a compromise. The lower house of the legislature, the House of Representatives, would have seats awarded by population. In the upper house, the Senate, each state would have two senators.

All the while, Madison sat scribbling away at his desk. Whenever he felt that a point needed clarification, he rose and addressed the assembly. Altogether, Madison spoke two hundred times during the convention. His point of view was not always upheld, however. Probably his greatest disappointment had to do with slavery. Madison had long disliked slavery, even though his father's plantation was dependent on slave labor. He sided with northern delegates at the convention in proposing that the slave trade be halted immediately, arguing that such trade was "dishonorable to the American character." A compromise with southern states was worked out, whereby the slave trade would continue until 1808. For the purpose of representation in Congress and the **electoral college**, a slave would be counted as three-fifths of a person. This plan is known as the Three-Fifths Compromise.

On September 17, 1787, the new constitution was signed. Madison's invaluable contribution to the convention had made him very respected. "Every person seems to acknowledge his greatness," William Pierce of Georgia said of Madison. "The affairs of the United States, he perhaps, has the most correct knowledge of, of any man in

George Washington, Benjamin Franklin, and others signing the Constitution in Philadelphia on September 17, 1787.

the Union." For his work in planning the convention and creating a blueprint for a new government, James Madison has been known ever since as the Father of the Constitution.

Next, it was up to the individual states to **ratify**, or approve, the new constitution. In a campaign to convince the state legislatures, Madison, Alexander Hamilton, and John Jay wrote a series of newspaper articles explaining the new form of government. Twenty-nine of the eighty-five essays were written by Madison. Known as *The Federalist* papers, they became the classic defense of the theory and philosophy of the Constitution. In June 1788, after nine states had ratified it, the Constitution became official law and the foundation of the U.S. government.

In the first election under the new Constitution in January 1789, Madison was elected to the House of Representatives. His first order of business was to write a series of amendments, or changes, to the Constitution. Critics of the Constitution charged that it did not clearly spell out the rights that belonged to the individual as opposed to the federal government. Now, drawing on his experience with the Virginia Declaration of Rights, Madison listed the natural rights of citizens: freedom of speech, religion, and the press, the right to **petition** and assemble, the right to bear arms, the right to trial by jury, and more. The first ten amendments that Congress passed are known as the Bill of Rights.

Still single, Madison was living in Philadelphia, the temporary seat of government. In the ten years since Kitty Floyd had jilted him, he had helped write the Constitution and found a nation. He had not, however, courted another woman. It was time to try his luck at love again.

# chapter TWO

# QUAKER GIRL

From the moment of her birth on May 20, 1768, their little girl brought love and joy into the lives of John and Mary Coles Payne of Guilford County, North Carolina. Perhaps that is why they gave her the playful name Dolley. The Paynes were members of the Society of Friends, also known as Quakers, a strict religious group that forbade dancing, playing cards, and wearing colorful or fancy clothes. As Quakers, they were also peace-loving, hospitable, and strong believers in equality and in the **abolition** of war and slavery. All her life, Dolley would be known for her sunny disposition, tolerant nature, and generosity of spirit.

Dolley Madison at twenty-six in a miniature by James Peale in 1794. Although Dolley grew up dressing in the modest Quaker style, she harbored a flair for fashion.

Dolley's family was originally from Virginia, and they moved back there in 1769. John Payne became such a successful farmer that by the time his daughter was ten, they were living on a 960-acre (about 388 hectares) tobacco plantation in Scotchtown. The hard-working, conscientious Paynes raised eight children and were leaders at the Cedar Creek Meeting house. They sent Dolley and her brothers and sisters to the local Quaker school to study religion, reading, writing, and mathematics.

When she was about nine, Dolley was given a piece of colorful jewelry by her grandmother Mary Payne, who was not a Quaker. Dolley was not allowed to wear jewelry because it was considered frivolous by the Society of Friends. Instead of giving it up, she hid the gift in a small bag hung beneath her plain gray dress and white neckerchief. One day the string around her neck broke, and the forbidden bauble was lost forever. Dolley would never forget that jewelry—or her feeling that she was being punished for the sin of vanity.

# Quakers

The Religious Society of Friends was founded in northern England in 1652 by preacher George Fox. Because Friends were said to "tremble at the word of the Lord," people mocked them as "Quakers." They believed in universal brotherhood and the equality of men and women before God and thought that the Inner Light, or spirit of God, existed in everyone. Quakers infuriated people by refusing to use titles, bow, or remove their hats in the presence of their social superiors. Their reading of particular passages of the Bible also led them to wear plain clothing and to become **pacifists**. The beliefs Quakers held were so different from those of other religious groups that they were mistreated in England and in the early British colonies. Then, in 1681, Quaker William Penn received a royal land grant and founded a colony based on the principles of toleration and religious freedom—Pennsylvania.

As managers of a tobacco plantation, the Paynes also owned slaves, who were needed to work the land. Although Quakers disapproved of slavery, a Virginia colonial law forbade the freeing of slaves. Not until 1782, with the close of the American Revolution, did **manumission**, though still discouraged, become legal. The Paynes immediately freed all their slaves. Unable to run a large plantation without unpaid workers, the Paynes chose to sell their property and move to Philadelphia, Pennsylvania, a city with a large and active Quaker population.

## A New Start

By the late 1700s, the "City of Brotherly Love" founded by Quaker William Penn had become the largest and most important city in the new United States. "I saw more people in my first half hour in Philadelphia," Dolley wrote later, "than I had in my whole life." Still wearing her prim gray dress, she gazed with wonder at the colorful outfits of fashionable Philadelphia ladies. The pretty, blue-eyed teenager soon enjoyed an active social life with other Quaker youths and attracted many admirers. A young lawyer

Slaves toil on a Virginia tobacco plantation. Many slaves were needed to tend plants, dry leaves, and transport crops to the market.

In 1800, Philadelphia was an exciting city where Dolley attended a variety of social functions.

named John Todd Jr. was especially attentive, but Dolley held back. She was not ready to get married yet.

Her father, unfortunately, did poorly in the new business he had started as a merchant. His venture failed, his debts mounted, and the Society of Friends, which disapproved of owing money, expelled him for "failure to pay his debts." Following the advice of his conscience, John Payne had lost not only his fortune but also his faith. A broken man, he never recovered.

Her father's change in status prompted Dolley, then twenty-one, to accept the hand of John Todd in marriage. According to Quaker tradition, they announced their intention to wed three times in Meeting. On January 7, 1790, they stood up together in front of the whole congregation and exchanged their vows. Apparently it was a happy marriage, and in 1792 Dolley had a son, John Payne Todd, whom they called Payne.

Aaron Burr, then a United States senator from New York, introduced Dolley to James Madison, who was seventeen years her senior.

Shortly after his namesake was born, Dolley's father died, and her mother was forced to take in boarders to support her family. In 1790, Philadelphia had become the temporary capital of the new nation, and government workers streamed into the city. One of Mary Payne's first boarders was Aaron Burr, a senator from New York, who became a good friend of the family. Another visitor, George Steptoe Washington, nephew of the president, eloped with Dolley's younger sister Lucy. Because George was not a Quaker, Lucy was formally banned from Meeting.

Dolley had no sooner given birth to another son in August 1793 than the city was devastated by a deadly yellow fever epidemic. John Todd, his parents, and Dolley's infant son all died. Dolley, too, fell desperately ill, but she was nursed back to health by her mother. When she recovered, she found herself a widow with a young son.

Although Dolley never considered herself beautiful, everyone else found her dark hair, peaches and cream complexion, and fine figure remarkable. At age twenty-six, she was so striking that when she walked down the street, her friend Elizabeth Collins remembered, "Gentlemen would station themselves where they could see her pass." Clearly, Dolley would not remain a widow for long. One of her admirers may have been Aaron Burr, whom she made her son's guardian in her will. Whatever his intentions, Burr was outmaneuvered when a friend asked for an introduction to the attractive widow.

Sometime in May 1794, Dolley received a message from Burr that took her breath away. Quickly she jotted a note to Elizabeth Collins: "Thou must come to me. Aaron Burr says that the great little Madison has asked to be brought to see me this evening."

# CAPITAL COUPLE

James Madison had never actually met Dolley Todd when he asked Aaron Burr to introduce them. He knew a lot about her, however, as they had both lived in Virginia and had friends in common. Certainly Dolley knew and respected the reputation of the man she called the Great Little Madison. That May evening, dressed in a mulberry satin gown and a lace cap, Dolley entertained James Madison and Aaron Burr in the parlor of her home. By the time Madison left, he was completely smitten.

The "Great Little Madison" who won Dolley's heart. Madison in turn had his sights set on the lovely Dolley.

## A Love Match

It was a whirlwind courtship. Within a month, James asked Dolley to marry him. News of their romance reached the ears of Martha Washington, wife of the president and Dolley's kin by marriage. Martha asked Dolley point-blank whether she was engaged to Madison, and Dolley, surprised, stammered that she did not know. "If it is so, do not be ashamed to confess it," Martha told her. "Rather be proud; he will make thee a good husband and all the better for being so much older. We both approve of it."

Dolley retreated to her sister's home in Virginia to make up her mind. Because James was not a Quaker, the decision to marry him meant leaving her religious community behind. Two months passed while James waited in great anxiety. Finally, she sent him a letter accepting his proposal. On August 18, 1794, he wrote an ecstatic reply: "I received some days ago your precious favor from Fredericksburg. I cannot express but hope you will conceive the joy it gave me."

On September 15, 1794, twenty-six-year-old Dolley and forty-three-year-old James were married. In the middle of the festivities, Dolley dashed off a note to her friend Elizabeth Collins. "In the course of this day I give my hand to the man who of all others I most admire," she wrote, and signed her name "Dolley Payne Todd." A few hours later, after the marriage ceremony, she returned to add a postscript: "Evening—Dolley Madison! Alas!"

Dolley may not have been in love when she married, but it did not take her long to fall very hard. James proved to be a doting husband and a good father to her young son, Payne, whom he adopted. Dolley and James would never have any children of their own.

Like her sister before her, Dolley was dismissed from the Society of Friends for marrying outside the faith. Yet she took her rejection in stride. For the rest of her life, Dolley would retain the Quaker virtues of tolerance, honesty, kindness, and generosity. Now, though, she could also indulge her craving for beauty, dressing in silks and satins, especially in her favorite color, bright yellow.

As a congressman's wife, Dolley did a lot of entertaining at the Madisons' three-story brick house in Philadelphia. She demonstrated that she could talk to practically anyone—even her husband's political opponents—about almost anything. Everyone was won over by her warm, friendly manner. "Politics," Dolley once confided to her sister, "is the business of men. I don't care what offices they hold, or who supports them. I care only about *people*."

## Politics in the New Nation

By the end of George Washington's first term in office, the country was divided into two political parties, the Democratic-Republicans and the Federalists. A Democratic-Republican, Madison stood with his best friend Thomas Jefferson in favoring the rights of state and local governments, agricultural interests, and civil rights. Even though he had worked with Federalist Alexander Hamilton to get the Constitution ratified, now he felt that Hamilton wanted to make the federal government too powerful. Hamilton and other

# The French Revolution

In July 1789, revolutionaries in France overthrew the nation's **monarchy** and established a **republic.** As the unrest increased, a radical group seized power and began a "Reign of Terror" that resulted in the massacres and executions of more than ten thousand French citizens, including King Louis XVI. Other European rulers, alarmed by the violence, raised armies to overthrow the revolutionaries. After years of successfully fighting off the forces of Great Britain, the Netherlands, Austria, and Prussia, an ambitious young general named Napoleon Bonaparte became **dictator** of France in 1800. His drive for world domination would launch Europe into another fifteen years of conflict.

Frustrated by social inequality and a lack of religious and cultural freedoms, revolutionaries attacked the Royal Palace during the French Revolution in 1789.

Federalists supported a strong central government, industry, banking, the shipping trade and leadership by a select few. Madison led the opposition against Hamilton's proposal for a national bank and making the federal government responsible for states' debts.

The political divide deepened with the onset of the French Revolution and the war between France and other nations in Europe. Great Britain began to seize U.S. ships and imprison American sailors. In response, President Washington sent John Jay

Dolley wears one of her signature empire-style dresses c. 1804.

to England to negotiate. The resulting treaty preserved peace, but it did not specify that Britain would stop attacking U.S. vessels. Madison felt strongly that Washington had sold out to Britain, and in the spring of 1796, he tried to kill Jay's Treaty in the House of Representatives. He lost by one vote, and lost, as well, the friendship of Washington.

After two terms, Washington decided not to run again, and the 1796 election went to Federalist John Adams. Madison did not seek reelection to Congress, and he and Dolley retreated to the country, where they enjoyed life at Montpelier for two years. Adams had only a one-term presidency, however, and with Thomas Jefferson's election as president in 1800, the Madisons were off to Washington, D.C., the new permanent capital. James Madison was appointed Jefferson's secretary of state in 1801.

At the start of the new century, Washington, D.C. was a raw, muddy town, full of scattered, half-completed homes and government buildings. The new President's House was large, damp, and mostly empty. Because Thomas Jefferson's wife, Martha, had died in 1782, Dolley often served as his hostess. She presided with grace, able to make everyone feel comfortable and at ease.

By then, Dolley had become known for the elegance of her wardrobe. She usually wore empire-style dresses, with high waists and low necklines, which she accessorized with turbans or hair bands. At a state dinner, one observer noted that Dolley "had on her head a turban of white satin, with three large white ostrich feathers hanging over her face . . . her dress, too, of white satin . . . with large capes trimmed with swan's down, was rich and beautiful."

So great was Dolley's popularity that a French military official praised her as "one of [America's] most valuable assets."

One of Dolley's few critics was the wife of British ambassador Anthony Merry. Mrs. Merry was once mortified at a president's dinner when Jefferson defied proper etiquette and escorted Mrs. Madison into dinner instead of herself. Later, Mrs. Merry tried to get her revenge by sneering that a dinner at the Madisons' was more like a "harvest home supper than the entertainment of a Secretary of State." When she heard this, Dolley merely commented, "But abundance is preferable to elegance. . . . The profusion of my table, so repugnant to foreign customs, arises from the happy circumstance of abundance and prosperity in our country."

Napoleon Bonaparte in a portrait from 1812 by Jacques-Louis David.

## Foreign Matters

The Jefferson presidency was dominated by foreign policy problems. In 1800, a brilliant young general named Napoleon Bonaparte seized power in France and briefly ended hostilities with Britain. In secret, though, Napoleon was planning to conquer Europe and needed money. Therefore, in 1802, when Madison sent envoys to Paris to try to buy New Orleans and West Florida from France, Napoleon countered with an even more daring offer. He would sell them all of the vast Louisiana Territory— stretching from the Mississippi River to the Rocky Mountains—for a mere $15 million dollars! Jefferson and Madison realized this was a chance like no other and asked the Senate to approve the sale. The Louisiana Purchase doubled the size of the United States for three cents per acre (about 0.4 hectares).

By 1803, France and Britain were once again at war, and both nations interfered with U.S. trade. The British stopped U.S. ships from trading with France and **impressed** thousands of sailors on the ships they seized. The French were just as determined to keep the United States from trading with Britain. Between them, France and Britain seized hundreds of U.S. merchant ships and badly hurt the American shipping industry.

At Madison's urging, in 1807, Congress passed the Embargo Act, forbidding American merchants to trade with anyone. If U.S. ships never left a dock, the rationale went, they couldn't be seized, and European trade would be hurt. "Our trade is the most powerful weapon we can use in our defense," one Democratic-Republican paper proclaimed hopefully.

Madison and Jefferson soon found out, though, that the embargo harmed the U.S. economy more than it hurt the British and French. In the space of one year, exports plummeted from $108 million to $22 million. Sailors and their families starved; merchants went bankrupt, farmers could not sell their tobacco, grain, and cotton. Soon the country was in a **recession**.

Congress repealed the law on the day Jefferson left office. Instead, it passed the Nonintercourse Act, which prevented the United States from trading with only Britain and France.

Despite the failure of the embargo, the Democratic-Republicans remained the most popular political party in the country. When Jefferson announced that he was leaving office after two terms, he urged his friend James Madison to succeed him. Madison won the election of 1808 easily, defeating both his Federalist rival Charles Pinckney and a bid from a fellow Democratic-Republican, James Monroe. Pinckney later remarked that he was "beaten by Mr. and Mrs. Madison. I might have had a better chance had I faced Mr. Madison alone."

Madison took office in a troubled time. None of the disputes with Britain or France had been resolved. One false step, and the nation would be thrust into war.

# CHAPTER FOUR

# MR. PRESIDENT AND THE LADY PRESIDENTRESS

On March 4, 1809, James Madison was sworn in as the fourth president of the United States. "Mr. Madison was extremely pale and trembled excessively when he first began to speak," wrote Margaret Smith, wife of the editor of the Washington newspaper, the *National Intelligencer*, "but [he] soon gained confidence and spoke audibly."

At the reception afterward, Dolley easily stole the show. "She looked extremely beautiful," Smith gushed, "dressed in a plain cambrick dress with a very long train. . . . She was all dignity, grace, and affability." That evening, Dolley Madison hosted four hundred guests at the first inaugural ball to be held since the Washington administration. At the supper, Dolley demonstrated her diplomatic skills by seating herself between the French and English ambassadors.

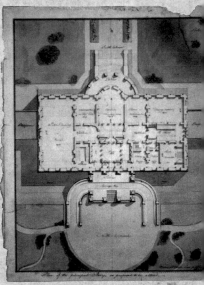

A drawing by Benjamin Latrobe outlining his architectural plans for the White House, 1807.

## At Home in the President's House

Dolley Madison's first priority was to decorate the President's House, left practically unfurnished by Thomas Jefferson. After she gave a group of congressmen a tour of the shabby residence, she was granted $5,000 to fix it up. She worked closely with noted architect Benjamin Latrobe for the job. He furnished the parlor (now the Red Room) in her favorite color, canary yellow. In the Elliptical Salon (now the Blue Room), he installed long red velvet curtains, red upholstered furniture, and cream wallpaper. George Washington's portrait was hung in the dining room, overlooking the buffet table where Dolley served lavish suppers and the new dessert craze, ice cream in warm pastry shells.

The "Lady Presidentress," as Dolley was known, presided over extremely popular Wednesday-afternoon receptions. New York writer Washington Irving wrangled an invitation when he was in town and left a perceptive eyewitness account of the scene: "In a few minutes I emerged from dirt and darkness into the blazing splendor of Mrs. Madison's drawing-room. Here I was most graciously received; found a crowded collection of great and little men, of ugly old women and beautiful young ones. . . . Mrs. Madison is a fine, portly buxom dame, who has a smile and a pleasant word for everybody."

Martha Washington's and Abigail Adams's receptions had been stiff, formal affairs. Instead of meeting her guests in a reception line, Dolley liked to circulate among them. Sometimes she offered people snuff from her gold-and-enamel snuffbox. Dolley was addicted to snuff, powdered tobacco that was sniffed up the nose. Sometimes she would carry a book, such as Miguel de Cervantes's *Don Quixote*, so that if all else failed, she could start a conversation about her reading.

## The Road to War

James, meanwhile, was working around the clock to stave off war. The Nonintercourse Act was not working, and French and British attacks on U.S. ships continued. With the largest Navy in the world, Britain needed an enormous fighting force, yet it continually lost seamen to U.S. ships. The United States, it seemed, paid its sailors better and did not whip them as often as did the British. American merchants could not afford to give up its extra hands, so the British kept boarding U.S. ships to get them back.

In May 1810, Madison tried yet again to use commercial pressure to affect foreign relations. He backed a plan submitted by a congressman named Nathaniel Macon that reversed the Nonintercourse Act. Under Macon's Bill Number 2, the United States

American sailors are impressed into the British Navy following the defeat of the USS *Chesapeake* by HMS *Leopold* on June 22, 1807.

would resume trade with both Britain and France. Yet as soon as one of these countries recognized U.S. **neutrality**, the United States would immediately stop trading with the other. Madison sat back and waited to see who would take the bait.

Napoleon, it seemed, was the one. On August 2, he sent word that he would respect U.S. neutrality. (He did not mention that he had already authorized the seizure of all foreign, including U.S., ships in the harbors of his empire.) Madison took Napoleon at his word and promptly announced to Britain that he was again suspending trade. The United States edged closer to war.

Many Americans, especially in the South and West, urged it on. Some Democratic-Republicans elected in the congressional elections of 1810 were "**War Hawks**," eager to declare war on Britain. They felt strongly that Britain was humiliating the United States by refusing to accept its rights on the high seas. "If we submit to Britain, the independence of this nation is lost," one congressman warned. War Hawks such as Henry Clay of Kentucky and John C. Calhoun of South Carolina thought war would give the United States an opportunity to seize Canada from the British. "The militia of Kentucky are alone [able] to place Montreal and Upper Canada at your feet," Clay declared to Congress.

War Hawks also suspected that the British were behind the Native American unrest along the frontier. As settlers pressed west into the Northwest Territory of present-day Ohio, Illinois, and Indiana, they tried to pressure American Indians into signing treaties giving up their land. Many Native Americans fought back instead, sometimes with British weapons they had traded for fur. War Hawks cried that the British were arming the American Indians.

The prospect of war split the country. In New England, where the livelihood of merchants and seamen depended on overseas trade, Federalists wanted to settle with Britain at any cost. In the South and West, War Hawks clamored for war, while other Democratic-Republicans were not so sure. Madison began to

Henry Clay of Kentucky was a prominent War Hawk who pushed for territorial expansion and war with Great Britain.

ready the country for what he thought was inevitable. In November 1811, he called for the enlistment of 25,000 troops, the preparation of the Navy for sea duty, and the arming of merchant vessels. He dispatched a ship, the *Hornet*, to Britain with the news that the United States was arming. If the British did not reverse their position on neutrality, war would result.

"I think there will be war," Dolley confided to her sister Anna. Just in case, she ordered a large shipment of clothes from Paris, "large head-dresses, a few flowers, feathers, gloves and stockings, black and white, and any other pretty things."

The *Hornet* returned on May 19, 1812, with the news that the British government had not changed its position. Congress voted for war, and on June 18, Madison signed the declaration.

Its supporters would call the War of 1812 the "Second War of American Independence." To James Madison's political foes, however, it would be known sarcastically as "Mr. Madison's War."

## Tecumseh and the Battle of Tippecanoe

As thousands of U.S. settlers pushed west after the American Revolution, they took over traditional Native American territory. A Shawnee warrior named Tecumseh tried to unite the various Native American nations into a confederation to resist the settlers. With his brother, Tenskwatawa, or the Prophet, Tecumseh and his followers founded a village called Prophetstown on Tippecanoe Creek in Indiana Territory. William Henry Harrison, governor of the territory, took advantage of Tecumseh's absence on a recruiting mission to march one thousand militiamen toward the village. Though Tecumseh had warned his brother not to fight the whites, on the night of November 7, 1811, Tenskwatawa and about six hundred Native Americans surprised Harrison's camp. Though neither side decisively won the Battle of Tippecanoe, the militia destroyed Prophetstown and weakened Tecumseh's dream of an Indian Confederation. Tecumseh and his followers went to Canada to fight on the side of the British in the War of 1812.

Shawnee leader Tecumseh died at Battle of the Thames on Oct. 18, 1813. With him died Native Americans' best hope for unification.

# CHAPTER FIVE

# LEADERS IN WAR

The United States was unprepared for war. There were only sixteen ships in the U.S. Navy, in comparison to Britain's nearly eight hundred warships. The British, however, were so involved in the European struggle against Napoleon that they could not turn their full attention to the conflict on the other side of the Atlantic. War Hawks planned to make a surprise raid on Canada before Britain could send more troops or ships to North America. Thomas Jefferson confidently proclaimed, "The acquisition of Canada this year [1812] will be a mere matter of marching." Many people thought that the Canadians were as eager to gain independence from Britain in 1812 as the thirteen original colonies had been in 1776.

U.S. general William Hull ponders whether to surrender Fort Detroit to the British on August 16, 1812. When he did, he was convicted on charges of neglect of duty and cowardice and sentenced to be shot. In light of Hull's age and his heroism during the Revolutionary War, however, James Madison spared his life.

First, though, the U.S. forces had to get into Canada. An aging and incompetent general named William Hull crossed into Canada with twenty-five thousand men but turned back when the Canadians tricked him into thinking that enemy forces were far larger than expected. Tecumseh, a Native American warrior who had been made a general by the British government, led his men on raids against the invaders. Then, when the Canadian forces followed Hull back across the border to Fort Detroit, in present-day Michigan, he surrendered without firing a shot on August 16, 1812. Madison was appalled.

Surprisingly, the greatest victories of the early war turned out to be at sea. Despite the small size of the U.S. Navy, it boasted six "superfrigates" designed during George Washington's administration. Able to carry up to fifty-four guns and four hundred and fifty men, the superfrigates were faster, more flexible, and better armored than the warships of other nations. One of them, the USS *Constitution*, encountered the British frigate *Guerriere* off Newfoundland on August 19, 1812. After Captain Isaac Hull (nephew of the general) maneuvered the *Constitution* close to the side of the British ship, its cannon blasted into the *Guerriere*, striking off all of its masts. Its stunning success earned the *Constitution* the nickname Old Ironsides.

## Campaigns on Land and Sea

This and other victories at sea gave Madison's 1812 reelection campaign a much-needed boost. Madison was convinced, as he wrote Jefferson, that the election would "bring the popularity of the war, or of the administration, or both, to the *experimentum crusis* [decisive test]." It was a vicious campaign, characterized by personal attacks on Madison and his administration. Federalists had so little support outside of New England, however, that they were forced to nominate an antiwar Republican from New York, DeWitt Clinton, for the presidential slot. It was a competitive race—128 electoral votes for Madison, 89 for Clinton—but Madison would stay in.

Neither the British nor the U.S. forces had a decisive advantage in the war by spring 1813. By then the British had established a **blockade** of U.S. ports along the Atlantic. As Captain James Lawrence sailed the frigate USS *Chesapeake* out of Boston Harbor, it was set upon by the British *Shannon*, and Lawrence was mortally wounded. Even though the U.S. Navy lost the battle, Lawrence's last, defiant words, "Don't give up the ship," became a Navy slogan. On land, the U.S. troops invaded Canada again and burned public buildings in the village of York (now Toronto). British admiral Sir George Cockburn retorted that now he would march into Washington and burn down the President's House.

His threats reached the Madisons in Washington. In May, Dolley wrote to Madison's secretary Edward Coles, "One of our generals has discovered a plan of the British,—it is to land as many chosen rogues as they can about 14 miles [22 km] below Alexandria, in the night, so that they may be on hand to burn the President's House and offices. I do not tremble at this, but I feel hurt that the admiral . . . should send me word that he would make his bow at my drawing-room very soon."

Captain James Lawrence was mortally wounded during the battle between his ship, the USS *Chesapeake,* and HMS *Shannon* on June 1, 1813. While dying he shouted, "Tell the men to fire faster and not to give up the ship; fight her till she sinks!" Inspired, every officer on the *Chesapeake* fought until either killed or wounded.

Then, on June 13, Madison fell ill. For a time, he hovered between life and death. "It has been three weeks since I have nursed him night and day," Dolley wrote. "Sometimes I despair!" While he was recovering, Madison learned that the U.S. Navy had achieved a notable victory against the British Navy on Lake Erie. In September 1813, Captain Oliver Hazard Perry and his fleet captured an entire British squadron. "We have met the enemy," Perry messaged General William Henry Harrison triumphantly, "and they are ours."

Inspired, General Harrison retook Detroit and then crossed Lake Erie on Perry's ships to meet the British and Native Americans at Thames River, Canada, on October 5, 1813. In the fighting that day, Tecumseh died—and with him died the American Indians' hopes for a confederation. In the course of the next year, British and U.S. forces engaged in an inconclusive struggle along the Canadian border, with neither side able to retain control of territory it won in individual battles.

In April 1814, Napoleon surrendered in Europe, and Britain was free to concentrate on its troublesome former colonies. British troops remained anchored in the Chesapeake Bay, waiting for reinforcements. As the tension grew, the Madisons received anonymous threats from people who opposed the war. "Among other exclamations and threats," wrote Dolley to Hannah Gallatin, the wife of the secretary of the treasury, "they say, if Mr. M, attempts to move from this house, in case of an attack, they will stop him; and that he shall *fall with it*. I am determined to stay with him."

## Crisis in Washington

On August 18, 1814, approximately four thousand British troops landed and began marching north toward Washington. Resistance melted away, as inexperienced militia badly led by incompetent generals under the leadership of Secretary of War John Armstrong put up little resistance.

Alarmed, people began to flee the city on August 22. After ordering that important state papers—including the Declaration of Independence and the Constitution—be sent to Virginia for safe-keeping, Madison rode out to be with the army. For four days, sixty-three-year-old Madison would conduct the war on horseback, rarely resting or sleeping. Throughout, he remained calm and in control.

Dolley assured her husband she would be all right until he returned. She was left alone in the mansion with a few servants and a guard of one hundred men around the house. By the next day, the guard had disappeared, and James sent her a message to be ready to leave at a moment's notice. Hurriedly, Dolley packed important papers, along with a few clothes. From an upstairs window, she looked through a spyglass at the hordes of Washingtonians swarming down Pennsylvania Avenue on their way to Virginia.

The night of August 23, James arrived home again for a brief visit. The couple was roused at midnight by an urgent message from James Monroe: "The enemy are in full march on Washington." Toward dawn on August 24, they climbed up on the roof with the spyglass and searched the horizon for signs of approaching troops.

At daylight, James left again after asking Dolley to have the table set for dinner. He hoped to be back with some **cabinet** officers at about 3:00 P.M. At a meeting with his top military command, Madison gave an order to Commodore Joshua Barney to remove the guns from his gunboats and transport them to the front at

# The British Are Coming

Stranded in the President's House while the British advanced toward Washington, D.C., Dolley Madison wrote her sister Lucy a long letter that provided a running commentary on her situation. The following excerpt is from Wednesday, August 24, 1814:

"Three o'clock

Will you believe it, my sister? We have had a battle or skirmish near Bladensburg, and I am still here, within sound of the cannon! Mr. Madison comes not; may God protect him! Two messengers covered with dust come to bid me fly; but I wait for him. . . . At this late hour a wagon has been procured; I have had it filed with the plate and most valuable portable articles belonging to the house; whether it will reach its destination, the bank of Maryland, or fall into the hands of British soldiery, events must determine. Our kind friend, Mr. Carroll, has come to hasten my departure, and is in a very bad humour with me because I insist on waiting until the large picture of George Washington is secured, and it requires to be unscrewed from the wall. This process was found too tedious for these perilous moments; I have ordered the frame to be broken, and the canvas taken out; it is done,—and the precious portrait placed in the hands of two gentlemen from New York, for safe keeping.

And now, dear sister, I must leave this house, or the retreating army will make me a prisoner in it, by filling up the road I am directed to take. When I shall see or write you, or where I shall be tomorrow, I cannot tell!"

Bladensburg, Maryland. Then, Madison remounted his horse and rode about 8 miles (13 km) to the battlefield. There he watched as raw American troops fled before experienced redcoats. "The militia men ran like sheep chased by dogs," one observer said. Only Barney and his seamen stuck to their guns, firing until their ammunition ran out.

Dolley could hear the cannons, too. As one messenger after another rushed into the President's House and warned her to go, she packed the silver, some books, and her red velvet draperies. Then, at the last minute, she had Washington's portrait removed from the dining room wall and rolled up. When two visitors from New York appeared to ask if they could be of assistance, she instructed them to bring the portrait, the papers, and some eagle ornaments to a farm in the country. Giving one final glance around her beautifully decorated home, Dolley stepped into her carriage and departed. A spectator saw "Mrs. Madison in her carriage flying full speed . . . accompanied by an officer carrying a drawn sword."

Members of the White House staff hurry to escape the British attack on Washington, D.C., in 1814 as Dolley pauses to save Gilbert Stuart's priceless portrait of George Washington.

As planned, she rendezvoused with some friends in Georgetown, then left with them for Virginia.

Forced to retreat, James rushed back to the mansion, reaching it just after 3:00 P.M., only to find that Dolley had left before him. He, too, left for Virginia. For the rest of the afternoon and into the evening, James, Dolley, and their parties crisscrossed the northern Virginia countryside, searching for and missing each other in the gathering dark. James spent much of the night on horseback, searching for his wife. Dolley finally found a home where she could rest.

On the Madisons' heels, the British marched into Washington. At 9:00 P.M. that evening, they staged a mock vote in the House of Representatives and agreed to set fire to the city. The Capitol, the Navy Yard, the Library of Congress, and many other government buildings were torched. "No drawing room was ever as brilliantly lit as the whole city that night," an observer recalled. "As flames burst through the roof of the Capitol, there was a roll of thunder."

At 10:30 P.M., Admiral Cockburn and a group of redcoats entered the President's House. Cockburn sat down at the dining room table, still set for dinner, and raised a wine glass into the air. "To Jemmy Madison's health!" he toasted his absent host. Then, after grabbing some souvenirs—Madison's hat, Dolley's seat cushion, a sword, some love letters—the redcoats left, tossing lit torches through the windows on their way out.

In Virginia, James and Dolley Madison watched the reddening sky from their separate vantage points. The city of Washington was burning.

The next morning, August 25, 1814, the British resumed their arson. Suddenly a mighty storm came up—some said it was a hurricane—that knocked down people and trees and tore the roofs off buildings. Drenched and frightened, the British decided they had had enough. By sunrise the following day, all British troops had marched out of town and were on their way back to their ships.

Finally, Dolley and James met for a short visit at Wiley's Tavern in Virginia before going their separate ways again. After three days on the run, Dolley sneaked back into the city disguised as a countrywoman. The Madisons found the government buildings gutted and the President's House a smoldering ruin. After a short period at the home of Dolley's sister Anna, the Madisons moved into the Octagon House, an elegant residence owned by a friend.

On September 11, the British fleet anchored below Baltimore and eight thousand troops went ashore. This time, however, the U.S. militia fought them off. For twenty-five hours, the British battered Fort McHenry in Baltimore Harbor with mortars and rockets. A young lawyer named Francis Scott Key watched the bombardment from a neighboring ship. When dawn broke, the U.S. "flag was still there," and Cockburn's ships were in retreat. Inspired, Key wrote a poem that later became the national anthem of the United States: "The Star-Spangled Banner."

A few days later, Madison learned that the U.S. forces had also routed a fleet of sixteen British warships and fifteen thousand troops at Plattsburg, New York, on Lake Champlain. Finally, the Madisons had cause for celebration.

British Admiral Sir George Cockburn in the chair of the speaker of the House of Representatives in the Capitol building during the British invasion of Washington, D.C., on August 24, 1814.

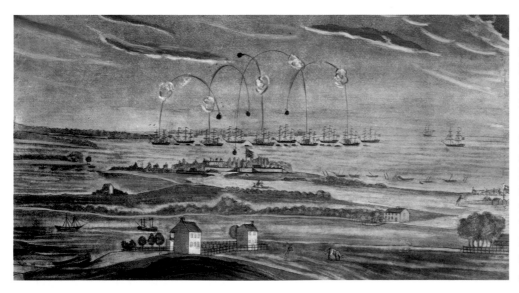

The valiant defense of the star-shaped Fort McHenry during the Battle of Baltimore, September 13–14, 1814, by one thousand dedicated Americans inspired Francis Scott Key to write "The Star-Spangled Banner." The defenders of Fort McHenry stopped the British advance on Baltimore.

Peace talks had actually been under way since August in Ghent, Belgium. Yet in October, Madison was dismayed to learn that the British were launching yet another attack, this time on New Orleans, Louisiana. So confident were the British of ultimate victory that they proposed giving all the Northwest Territory—everything north of the Ohio River—to the Native Americans and parts of New York and New England to Canada.

Madison was also under fire from New England Federalists, who met at Hartford, Connecticut, in December 1814, to oppose the war. Some of the more radical delegates even muttered that if the war continued, the New England states would consider **secession** and make a separate peace treaty with England.

Between the war news and the news from New England that winter, Madison looked "miserably shattered and woebegone . . . in short broken-hearted" as one observer noticed. As the new year of 1815 was ushered in, the Madisons waited with the rest of the country for news of New Orleans.

The Battle of New Orleans took place on January 8, 1815, but word of its outcome did not reach Washington, D.C., until February 4. General Andrew Jackson, with half as many troops as the British, mowed down the British soldiers who attacked the U.S. trenches in a full frontal assault. Altogether, the British suffered more than two thousand casualties, the U.S. troops, just seventy-one. Jackson had won a spectacular victory.

Then, just ten days later, on February 14, a coach barreled along Pennsylvania Avenue with the best news of all—a peace treaty had arrived! The Treaty of Ghent had actually been signed in Europe on December 24—fifteen days before the Battle of New Orleans. It stipulated that everything could go back to the way it was before the war. In the words of John Quincy Adams, one of the peace commissioners at Ghent, "nothing was adjusted, nothing was settled." Madison signed the treaty that night, and the Senate ratified it the next day. The war was over.

British and American diplomats signing the Treaty of Ghent on December 24, 1814. Great Britain agreed to give up claims to the Northwest Territory, and both countries pledged to work toward ending the slave trade. America, in turn, gained influence as a foreign power.

## Peace at Last

The United States had proved that it could hold its own against the greatest military power on earth. Writing to his government, French ambassador Louis Serurier perceptively commented that the war had "given the [U.S. people] what they so essentially lacked, a national character founded on a glory common to all." A wave of nationalism swept the country.

Madison rode a crest of popularity but he did not seek reelection. In the last year and a half of his administration, Madison was a well-liked and respected president. Finally, the man who had envisioned and defended the Constitution could look once again to his nation's future. Madison proposed a new national bank, a national university, a uniform national currency, and an enlarged Navy. Under his direction, Washington was rebuilt. To replace the burned Library of Congress, Thomas Jefferson donated his personal library. The President's House, now a blackened stone shell, was slowly renovated, and the exterior was painted white. In time, it would be called the White House.

Dolley and James would never live in the house again, however. After a year in the Octagon House, they moved to a smaller residence on the corner of Nineteenth Street and Pennsylvania Avenue, so close to the road that passersby could peer in the windows. Every day, children would gather on the sidewalk to watch Dolley, dressed in her trademark turban, feed her pet parrot. At Easter, she organized an egg roll on the hill behind the U.S. Capitol, a tradition that continues today at the White House. She continued to entertain, hosting crowded dinners and receptions, dressed in fantastic, one-of-a-kind creations. At the 1816 Assembly Ball, people stood on benches to catch a glimpse of her in a black velvet gown and a gold lace turban. Dolley's last year as Lady Presidentress was her most brilliant social season ever.

Dolley's son Payne, who had been with the peace commissioners in Ghent, came back from Europe in debt, with French clothes and French manners and no plans for his future. The Madisons tried to persuade him to attend Princeton as his stepfather had done, but Payne protested that at age twenty-four he was too old. Instead, he would accompany his parents back to Montpelier, where perhaps he could settle down to the life of a country squire.

In March 1817, Madison's old friend and secretary of state, James Monroe, was sworn in as the fifth president. Madison left office in a shower of praise. "Notwithstanding a thousand faults and blunders," John Adams wrote to Thomas Jefferson, "[Madison's administration] has acquired more glory, and established more union; than all his three predecessors . . . put together." The Madisons were so beloved that they attended balls and receptions in their honor for a full month after Monroe's inauguration.

Then they took a steamboat down the Potomac to Virginia. A friend who accompanied them said of Madison, "If ever man rejoiced sincerely in being freed from the cares of public life it was he. During the voyage he was as playful as a child; talked and joked with everybody on board, and reminded me of a schoolboy on a long vacation."

James Monroe, fifth president of the United States, and Madison were always close and worked together frequently.

# HOME AT LAST

James Madison was sixty-six years old and Dolley was forty-nine when they retired to Virginia. Over the years, they had enlarged and improved Montpelier, adding two large wings and a columned walkway. Now, in the mornings, they could sit on the porch and look out on the rolling Blue Ridge Mountains far in the distance. For the next nineteen years, James and Dolley enjoyed a peaceful life together.

Madison, whom Jefferson called the "best farmer in the world," tried hard to make his plantation profitable again, experimenting with different crops and the newest plows and growing techniques. He became president of the Albemarle Agricultural Society and spent his time pondering farming questions, such as how to prevent black rot and how to keep squirrels out of corn.

James Madison three years before he died. Portrait by Asher Durand.

Often, James and Dolley would ride over to Charlottesville to visit Thomas Jefferson at his Monticello estate. Jefferson involved Madison in the overriding mission of his last years, the attempt to create the University of Virginia. Madison contributed money, helped plan the curriculum, and served on the board of visitors. Before Jefferson died on July 4, 1826—the fiftieth anniversary of the signing of the Declaration of Independence—he asked his old friend to "take care of me when dead, and be assured that I shall leave you with my last affections." After Jefferson's death, Madison

Dressed in one of her signature turbans, Dolley Madison is featured in this painting by Ezra Ames, c. 1817.

inherited his friend's gold-headed cane and took over for him as rector, or head, of the university.

Dolley bloomed in retirement, surrounded by nieces and nephews and occupied with reading, gardening, and entertaining. "She certainly has always been, and still is, one of the happiest of human beings," Margaret Smith wrote when she visited Dolley at Montpelier. "Time seems to favor her as much as fortune. She looks young and she says she feels so. I can believe her, nor do I think she will ever look or feel like an old woman."

Dolley was responsible for the hundreds of guests who came to Montpelier to see the former president, sometimes staying for three to four weeks at a time. James enjoyed the company. "He was a man of wit, relished wit in others, and his small bright blue eyes would twinkle wickedly," a guest recalled, "when lighted up by some whimsical composition or exposition."

Yet for the Madisons, rich in land but not in money, entertaining was a constant drain on their shaky finances. Another worry was Payne, now a full-grown man who still showed no signs of settling down with a family and assuming his responsibilities as Madison's heir. He drank, he gambled, and he ran up huge debts that Madison tried to cover without alarming his wife.

Aware that he was in danger of going bankrupt, from 1821 on Madison devoted himself to editing his enormous correspondence and notes on the Constitutional Convention. He thought his papers were his most valuable family heirloom and hoped their sale would support Dolley after he had gone. Though his eyesight was failing, with Dolley's help he worked quietly on. By 1835, when English author Harriet Martineau visited Montpelier, eighty-four-year-old James Madison was the last Founding Father—the only member of the Constitutional Convention—left alive. He had "an uncommonly pleasant countenance," Martineau wrote of Madison later. His mind, she was happy to report, had lost none of its power, and his "relish for conversation could never have been keener."

On June 28, 1836, Madison's niece Nelly was in his room as his breakfast tray was brought in. He raised his spoon as if to eat, then put it down. "What is the matter, Uncle James?" Nelly asked.

"Nothing, my dear, but a change of mind," he answered. His head dropped, and he died. Among her husband's papers, Dolley found a last recommendation to his country: "The advice nearest to my heart and deepest in my convictions is that the Union of the States be cherished and perpetuated."

Dolley turned to the task James had assigned her, the publication of his papers. In March 1837, Congress voted to acquire the first half for the sum of $30,000. Of this, Dolley was able to keep only $9,000 after she had settled her husband's will. Then, she decided to return to Washington, which she had always missed. She felt, she said, as if she had "awakened after a dream of twenty years." Accompanied by her niece Anna and leaving Montpelier under the care of Payne, she moved to a small house on Lafayette Square.

## The *First* First Lady

As if she had never left, Dolley immediately regained her position as head of Washington society. For widower President Martin van Buren, she acted as sometime hostess; for Julia Tyler and Sarah Polk, wives of Presidents John Tyler and James K. Polk, she served as guide and advisor. Her New Year's Day and Fourth of July receptions were legendary. No one minded that her dress was out of date or that the dark curls peeking out from her old-fashioned turbans were false. Dolley, who had lost none of her zest for life, entertained the younger generation with stories of Washington, Jefferson, and the early republic. They were fascinated.

Dolley was always invited to government events—inaugurations, balls, and naval reviews. She was present at the Capitol with Samuel F. B. Morse when the first telegraph message was sent. She laid the cornerstone for the Washington Monument on July 4, 1848. In special recognition, Congress gave her a permanent pass to the House of Representatives, the first woman to be given that honor.

Dolley Madison in a daguerreotype, an early kind of photograph. By Mathew Brady, c. 1848.

As time went on and Congress delayed the purchase of the second half of Madison's papers, Dolley began to go broke. Her son Payne, ruined by drink, managed Montpelier so badly that Dolley finally had to sell it. She lived so frugally that good friends sometimes sent her baskets of food. Finally, when Dolley was eighty years old and on the verge of selling her silverware in order to live, Congress bought the remaining papers for $25,000.

A year later, on July 12, 1849, she died quietly in her sleep. Hundreds of Washingtonians attended her funeral, from President Zachary Taylor and his cabinet to members of Congress, the Supreme Court, and the military. Dolley had witnessed the first fifty years of the United States and known twelve presidents personally. In his eulogy, Taylor gave Dolley Madison the title by which all presidents' wives have been known since. "She will never be forgotten," the president said, "because she was truly our First Lady for a half-century."

# TIME LINE

| 1751 | James Madison Jr. is born on March 16 |
|------|---------------------------------------|
| 1768 | Dolley Madison is born on May 20 |
| 1771 | James Madison graduates from the College of New Jersey at Princeton |
| 1775 | James is appointed a colonel in the Orange County militia |
| 1776 | James becomes a delegate to the Virginia Constitutional Convention; Declaration of Independence is signed on July 4 |
| 1777 | James runs for a seat in the new Virginia House of Delegates in April |
| 1780 | James becomes a delegate to the Continental Congress |
| 1783 | Dolley and her family move to Philadelphia. Treaty of Paris ends the Revolutionary War on April 15 |
| 1787 | Constitutional Convention begins on May 25 |
| 1789 | James is elected to the House of Representatives |
| 1790 | Dolley Payne marries John Todd on January 7 |
| 1792 | John Payne Todd is born on February 29 |
| 1793 | William Temple Todd born in late summer; John Todd and William Temple Todd die in yellow fever epidemic in October |
| 1794 | James and Dolley marry on September 15 |
| 1801 | James is appointed secretary of state under Thomas Jefferson; James and Dolley move to Washington, D.C. |
| 1803 | Louisiana Purchase is signed |
| 1808 | James is elected president of the United States |
| 1811 | Battle of Tippecanoe occurs on November 7; U.S. militia destroys Prophetstown |
| 1812 | United States declares war on Great Britain on June 18; James is elected president for a second term |
| 1813 | The United States defeats Britain in Battle of Lake Erie and at the Thames River |
| 1814 | British burn Washington, D.C., on August 24. Treaty of Ghent ends War of 1812 on December 24 |
| 1815 | General Andrew Jackson defeats the British at Battle of New Orleans on January 8 |
| 1816 | James Monroe is elected president |
| 1817 | James and Dolley move back to Montpelier |
| 1836 | James Madison dies on June 28 |
| 1837 | Dolley returns to Washington, D.C. |
| 1844 | Dolley sells Montpelier |
| 1849 | Dolley Payne Todd Madison dies on July 12 |

# GLOSSARY

**abolition**—the act of outlawing slavery.

**blockade**—the blocking of a place, usually by ships, in order to prevent people or goods from moving in or out.

**boycott**—to be part of a group that refuses to have dealings with an organization, person, or business to protest or to force them into acceptance.

**cabinet**—officials who head government departments and who also meet to advise the president.

**dictator**—ruler who has supreme and total authority, especially one who has seized power or who uses it harshly or selfishly.

**electoral college**—group of people chosen from each state that gives the official vote for the president of the United States.

**impress**—to force into military service, especially the navy.

**manumission**—to set free from slavery or bondage; liberate.

**militia**—army of untrained citizens who serve as soldiers during emergencies.

**minutemen**—American soldiers of the Revolutionary War, who were ready to fight on a minute's notice.

**monarchy**—a nation or government lead by or in the name of a ruler, such as a king, queen, or emperor.

**neutrality**—not taking any side in a conflict.

**pacifist**—one who opposes war and refuses to practice or acknowledge violence as a way of settling disputes.

**petition**—formal, written request by many people that is made to a person in authority.

**ratify**—to approve formally.

**recession**—period of reduced or declining economic activity.

**redcoats**—slang term for British soldiers.

**republic**—nation in which those who make the laws and run the government are elected by the people.

**secession**—to withdraw from or leave an organization, in this case referring to withdrawal from the United States.

**secretary of state**—the position of the head of the U.S. Department of State, established in 1789. The U.S. Department of State is in charge of foreign affairs.

**tyranny**—government in which a single person rules with complete power, usually in a harsh way.

**War Hawk**—member of the twelfth U.S. Congress (1811–1813) who supported war with Great Britain.

# FURTHER INFORMATION

## Further Reading

Collier, Christopher, and James Lincoln Collier. *Creating the Constitution: 1787*. Tarrytown, NY: Benchmark Books, 1998.

Flanagan, Alice K. *Dolley Payne Todd Madison*. New York: Children's Press, 1998.

Fritz, Jean. *The Great Little Madison*. New York: Putnam, 1998.

Gaines, Ann. *James Madison: Our Fourth President*. Chanhassen, MN: Child's World, 2001.

Gormley, Beatrice. *First Ladies: Women Who Called the White House Home*. Madison, WI: Turtleback Books, 2004.

Hakim, Joy. *From Colonies to Country: 1735–1791*. (A History of Us, vol. 3). New York: Oxford University Press, 2001.

Hakim, Joy. *The New Nation: 1789–1850*. (A History of Us, vol. 4). New York: Oxford University Press, 2002.

January, Brendan. *James Madison: America's Fourth President*. (Encyclopedia of Presidents). New York: Children's Press, 2003.

Kelley, Brent P. *James Madison: Father of the Constitution*. New York: Chelsea House, 2000.

Kent, Zachery. *James Madison: Creating a New Nation*. Springfield, NJ: Enslow, 2004.

Madison, Barbara, and Alex Tavoularis. *Father of the Constitution: A Story about James Madison*. Minneapolis: Lerner, 2003.

Mayo, Edith P. (ed.) *The Smithsonian Book of First Ladies: Their Lives, Times, and Issues*. New York: Henry Holt/Smithsonian Institution, 1996.

Pflueger, Lynda. *Dolley Madison: Courageous First Lady*. Springfield, NJ: Enslow, 1999.

Santella, Andrew. *The War of 1812*. New York: Children's Press, 2000.

Weatherly, Myra. *Dolley Madison: America's First Lady*. Greensboro, NC: Morgan Reynolds, 2003.

# FURTHER INFORMATION

## Places to Visit

Greensboro Historical Museum
*Dolley Madison: The Story of One of
America's Most Beloved First Ladies*
130 Summit Avenue
Greensboro, North Carolina 27401
(336) 373-2043

Independence Hall
Chestnut Street
Independence Mall
Philadelphia, Pennsylvania 19106
(800) 537-7676

James Madison's Montpelier
11407 Constitution Highway
Montpelier Station, Virginia 22957
(540) 672-2728

Smithsonian National Museum
of American History
14th St. and Constitution Ave., N.W.
Washington, D.C. 20013
(202) 633-1000

National Constitution Center
525 Arch Street
Independence Mall
Philadelphia, Pennsylvania 19106
(215) 409-6600

The National First Ladies' Library
Education and Research Center
205 Market Avenue South
Canton, Ohio 44702
(330) 452-0876

United States Capitol
Constitution Avenue
Washington, D.C. 20515
(202) 224-3121

USS *Constitution* Museum
Charlestown Navy Yard
Building 22
Boston, Massachusetts 02129
(617) 426-1812

White House
1600 Pennsylvania Avenue, N.W.
Washington, D.C. 20500
(202) 456-2121

## Web Sites

The Dolley Madison Project
www.moderntimes.vcdh.virginia.edu/
madison/

The First Ladies of the United States
of America
www.whitehouse.gov

Independence National Historical Park
www.nps.gov/inde

Internet Public Library, Presidents of
the United States (IPL POTUS)
www.ipl.org/div/potus/jmadison.html

James Madison's Montpelier
www.montpelier.org

The National First Ladies' Library
www.firstladies.org

The Papers of James Madison
www.virginia.edu/pjm

**About the Author**

Ruth Ashby has written many award-winning biographies and nonfiction books for children, including *Herstory*, *The Elizabethan Age*, and *Pteranodon: The Life Story of a Pterosaur*. She lives on Long Island with her husband, daughter, and dog, Nubby.